EXAMPLES from THIS BOOK

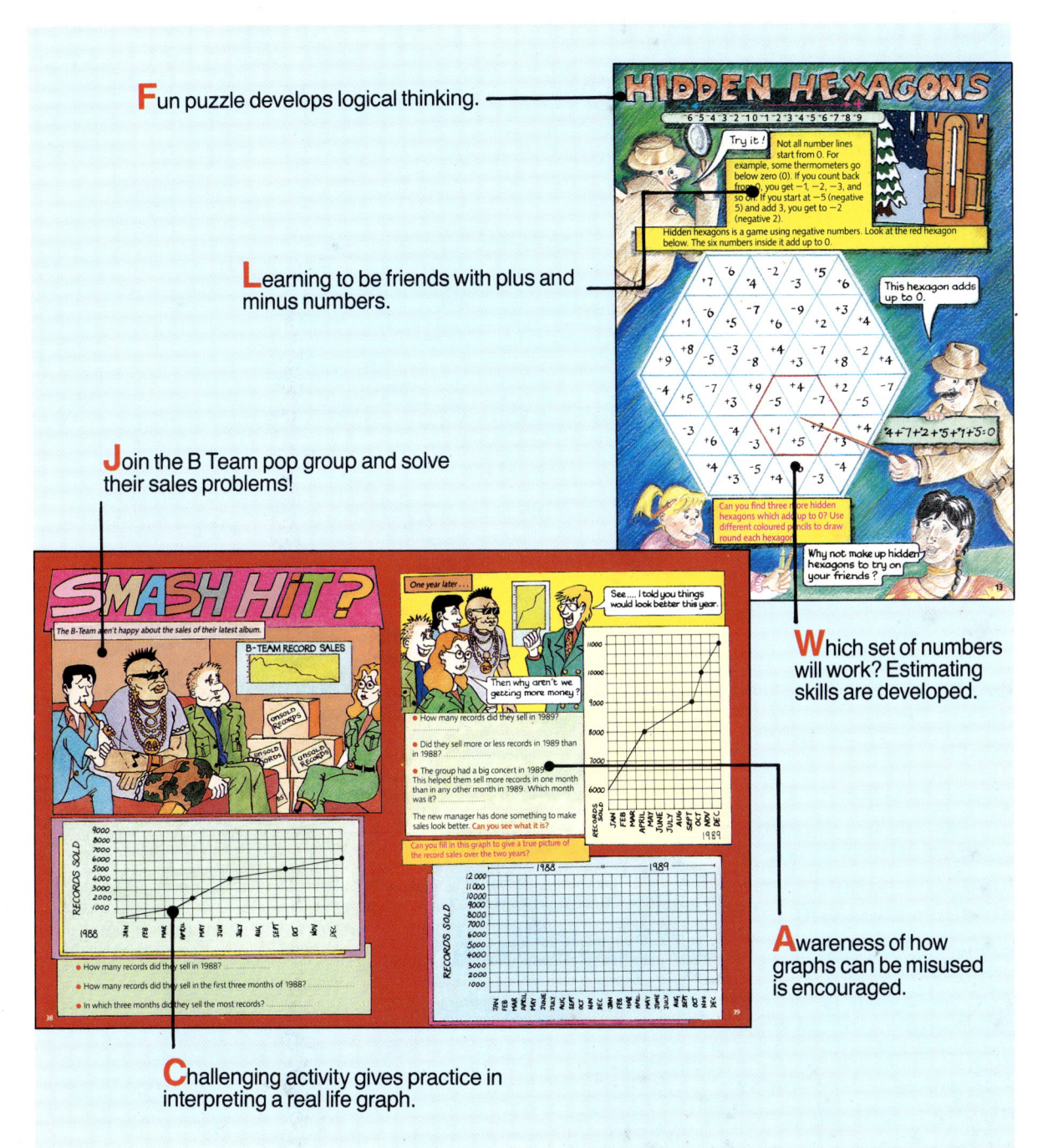

Fun puzzle develops logical thinking.

Learning to be friends with plus and minus numbers.

Join the B Team pop group and solve their sales problems!

Which set of numbers will work? Estimating skills are developed.

Awareness of how graphs can be misused is encouraged.

Challenging activity gives practice in interpreting a real life graph.

1

IN *this*

*M*aths is an essential part of our lives and our environment. We need to be able to use mathematical skills effectively and with confidence – such confidence can only come from understanding.

Maths 3 builds upon and extends the work done in the first two books. Learning to be friends with numbers and symbols is one of our major themes. We also stress throughout the importance of estimating, seeing connections, and being able to investigate solutions to practical real life problems.

At this level, the activities are more integrated, but they can be broadly divided into four main areas.

NUMBER

Central to the understanding of number is the 'feel' for the size of a number. Handling larger numbers and doing more complex operations are important at this stage. The calculator is vital for these and for developing logical thinking. Encourage your child to use their own calculator wherever possible.

These are some of the activities which emphasise handling number:

Amazing millions on page 8 gets your child thinking about just how big a million is – the activity involves estimating and calculating money, measure and time.

Gus and Hatchet's discount sale on page 26 involves calculating discounts and percentages – more complex operations for which a calculator is essential.

The darts competition on page 28 deals with much smaller numbers but demands logical thinking in order to decide who will play against who.

BOOK

MEASURE

Estimating measurements and being able to measure accurately are both vital everyday skills. Graphs are also concerned with measurement and scale. Being able to interpret the information given in graphs is an important aspect of real life maths.

These are some of the activities which provide practice in measurement:

The Great Bubble Gum Robbery on page 14 involves working out how Gus and Hatchet can make their getaway, using a simple map drawn to scale.

Cooking with Skulk on page 22 presents a recipe for cakes – accurate weighing and cooking will provide something truly edible – they even go down well in Gargoyle's Guest House!

SHAPE

In daily life, we frequently need to make decisions which involve spatial awareness, from packing for a holiday to designing and making shelves or cupboards.

Being able to think about and manipulate shapes is an important first step in the development of spatial awareness – an essential skill.

Pentominoes on page 19 will get your child thinking about shapes and experimenting with them.

Moving day for Tatty Tricia on page 40 encourages your child to help Tatty Tricia plan her new bedroom by moving scale drawings around on a plan. This involves investigating and making decisions on the best use of limited space.

LOGIC

Logical thinking underlies many of the activities in this book. At this stage in your child's development, logic becomes increasingly important in maths at school.

Queen of Hearts on page 21 uses a card game to encourage children to think logically about sequencing within sets.

Look also at these activities:
Match the pairs on page 12.
Stamps on page 35.

3

HOW THIS BOOK *works*

You can share in the fun of **Success!** If you want, you can do some of the activities with your child. But **Success!** does not depend on you. One of the benefits of the range is to encourage children to enjoy working independently, not just when the grown-ups are around.

YOU

have a special role to play. It's the one that comes naturally to any parent: give all the encouragement you can!

If you can give your child the benefits of more individual attention, there is no need for you to *teach* specific skills. **Success!** does not require specialist knowledge.

WHEN

you're ready to start on this book at home, sit down together and go through it. Talk about the activities and the zany characters and enjoy the often crazy situations. Start one or two activities to get the feel of them.

Then help to choose an activity to be completed and say that you'd like to see it when it's done.

HOW

will you know things are going well? When your child is absorbed, *thinking* about the activity and really *doing* the work, then you'll know that progress is being made. Look at the back of this book for further guidance.

Speed isn't important. Enjoyment and commitment are the telling signs.

WHAT

should your response be? Praise the results – don't criticise. If you think there is a better way of doing something, suggest it as an alternative, not as the only right way.

Make it clear that working at the activities is a good thing which brings praise. Effort does deserve recognition and it *will* bring results. Not least important, it will give confidence and increase enthusiasm for more activities and more learning.

Look out for opportunities to encourage work on other activities but go for short, frequent sessions – don't let it get boring!

Don't forget to *tick* off each completed activity on the *contents* page and share the sense of achievement and pleasure.

Success!

Maths 3

START HERE

I started this book on.........................

Name..

I finished it on ....

Pssst! It may look like a posh book but it's supposed to be written in — so do it!

Editorial and educational consultant

Dr. Roger Merry

ILLUSTRATORS:
Steve Brookes   Dave Parker
Matt Burke

Success! Contents

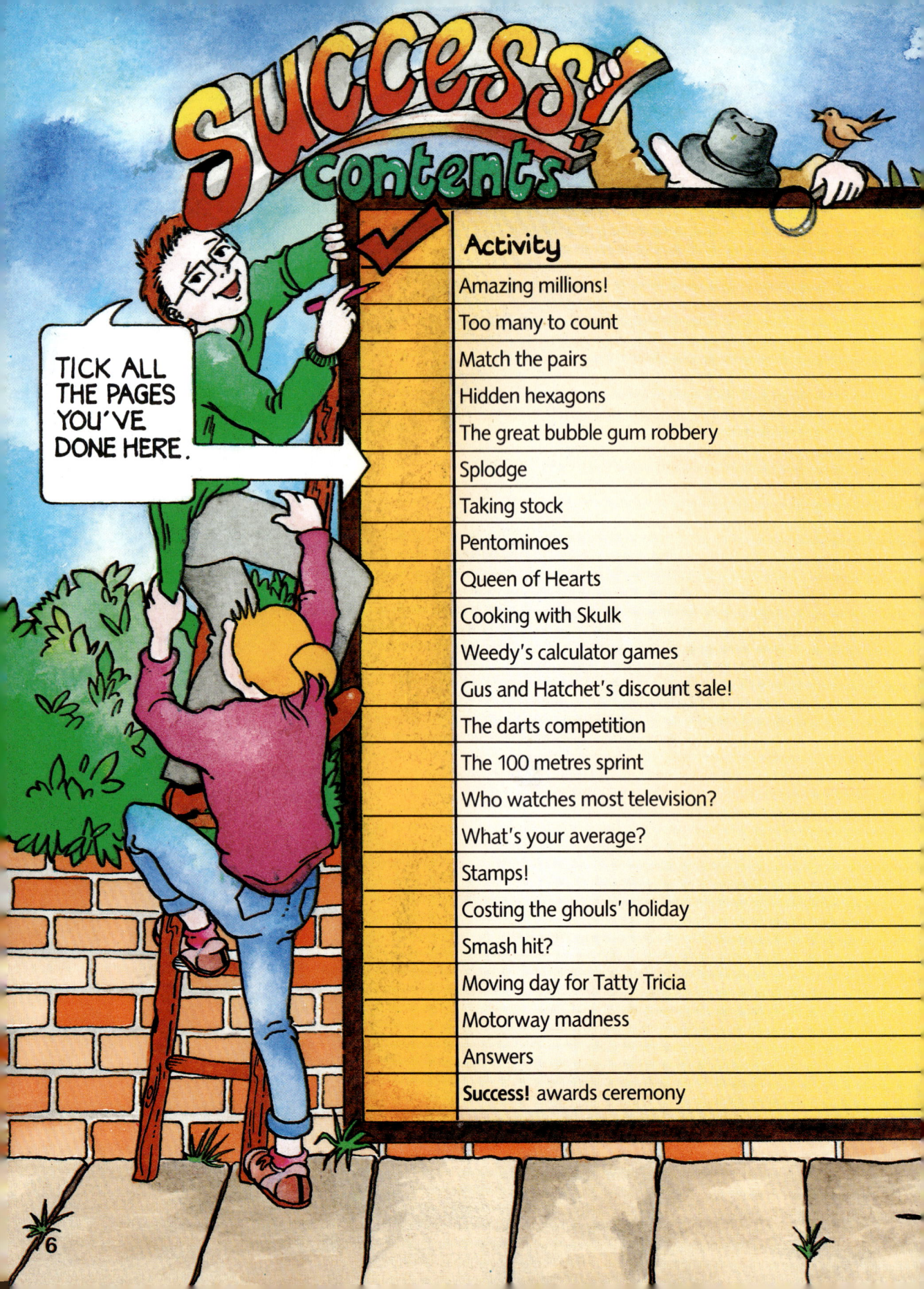

"TICK ALL THE PAGES YOU'VE DONE HERE."

✓	Activity
	Amazing millions!
	Too many to count
	Match the pairs
	Hidden hexagons
	The great bubble gum robbery
	Splodge
	Taking stock
	Pentominoes
	Queen of Hearts
	Cooking with Skulk
	Weedy's calculator games
	Gus and Hatchet's discount sale!
	The darts competition
	The 100 metres sprint
	Who watches most television?
	What's your average?
	Stamps!
	Costing the ghouls' holiday
	Smash hit?
	Moving day for Tatty Tricia
	Motorway madness
	Answers
	Success! awards ceremony

Maths Skills	Page no.
Estimating and calculating using a million	8
Estimating large numbers	10
Thinking logically; problem solving	12
Using plus and minus numbers to solve a puzzle	13
Interpreting a simple scale map	14
Using a calculator to work out simple accounts	16
Working out and rounding up quantities	18
Rearranging two dimensional shapes	19
Thinking logically; problem solving	21
Doubling weights and quantities	22
Practising the use of a calculator	24
Calculating percentages and discounts	26
Thinking logically; choosing numerical alternatives	28
Using two places of decimals	30
Calculating averages	32
Completing a chart to work out times and averages	34
Thinking logically; problem solving	35
Costing alternative holidays	36
Interpreting line graphs	38
Planning a room using scale drawings	40
Linking speeds, time and fuel consumption	44
	46
	47

AMAZING MILLIONS!

SID GENIUS'S MEMORY JOGGERS

1000 metres = 1 kilometre   1000 grams = 1 kilogram

1000 kilograms = 1 tonne

Millions H T U	Thousands H T U	H T U
1	0 0 0	0 0 0

H=Hundreds;   T=Tens;   U=Units

Gus and Hatchet tried to steal £1 000 000 in £1 coins. They had terrible problems carrying off all the money.

One £1 coin weighs only 9.3 g. How much does £1 000 000 weigh?

Estimate
930   tonnes
93   tonnes
9.3   tonnes

Draw a circle round the one you think is the correct weight.

Work out

£1 Coins	Weight
1	9.3 g
100	
1 000	
10 000	
100 000	
1 000 000	

Can you fill in the answers? Was your estimate right?

MARVELLOUS MINIS!

The Mini is Britain's most successful car. The first Minis were made in 1959. About 5 million have been sold since then.

Suppose just one million Minis set out from London one by one. Which city would the first one reach before the last one left London? Allow 10 metres for each Mini:

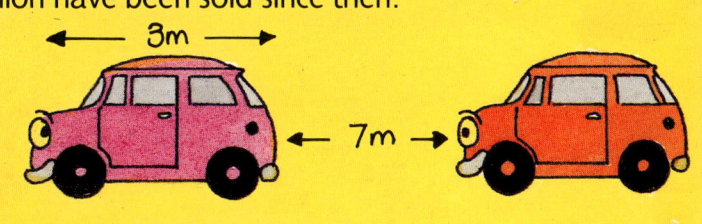

Estimate
Draw a circle in pencil round the city you think is the right one.

Work out
How many kilometres is it? Draw a circle round the city the first Mini will reach. Was your estimate right?

WORLD MAP

- Moscow (3000 km)
- London
- Peking (10 000 km)
- Tokyo (12 000 km)
- Paris (400 km)
- Bombay (9000 km)
- Rome (1900 km)

PLENTY OF PEOPLE!

In China a baby is born every second. How long before a million babies are born?

Estimate
In just under — 12 hours
12 days
12 weeks

Work out

Time	Babies born
1 second	1
1 minute	
1 hour	
1 day	
1 week	

Put a circle round the time you think is closest.

Can you work out how long it is before a million babies are born? Was your estimate right?

The population of the world is about 5000 million. It increases by 150 every minute. **How long before there are a million extra people in the world?**..

Can you find out about other 'amazing millions'?

TOO MANY

163, 164.......

What are you doing Weedy?

Which Mrs. Smith do you want? There are hundreds of Smiths in the telephone book!

Oh, I'm just counting how many people are called Smith.....

Look, there's a quicker way. How many *pages* of Smiths are there?

Oh, about 8.

And how many *columns* on each page?

Er......3.

And how many *names* in each column, roughly?

About 120.

Can you work out roughly how many Smiths there are in Weedy's telephone book?

On one page: 120 × .... = ...

on 8 pages: .... × .... = ...

It's not exact, of course. It's only an *estimate*. Now find a popular family name in your local telephone book. It might be Smith, Jones, Singh, or ....? Estimate how many of this family name there are altogether.

TO COUNT

Sid and Weedy are estimating how many cars go past their school each day.

Count how many cars go past in 10 minutes.

....38....39....

Can you help Sid and Weedy?

Weedy counted 39 cars in 10 minutes.
In one hour there are 6 × 10 minutes:
On one day there are 24 hours:
   Estimate for the whole day

39 × 6 × 24 = ...

I've just thought of a problem. This is rush hour. There won't always be so many cars on the road.

Can you estimate how many cars go past your school or house in one day? Think about times of the day when the traffic will be busy and when it will be quiet.

Use this way of estimating to work out roughly:

★ How much milk your family drinks in a year. ....

★ How many times you breathe in a year. ....

******! I forgot to ring Mrs. Smith!

11

MATCH THE PAIRS

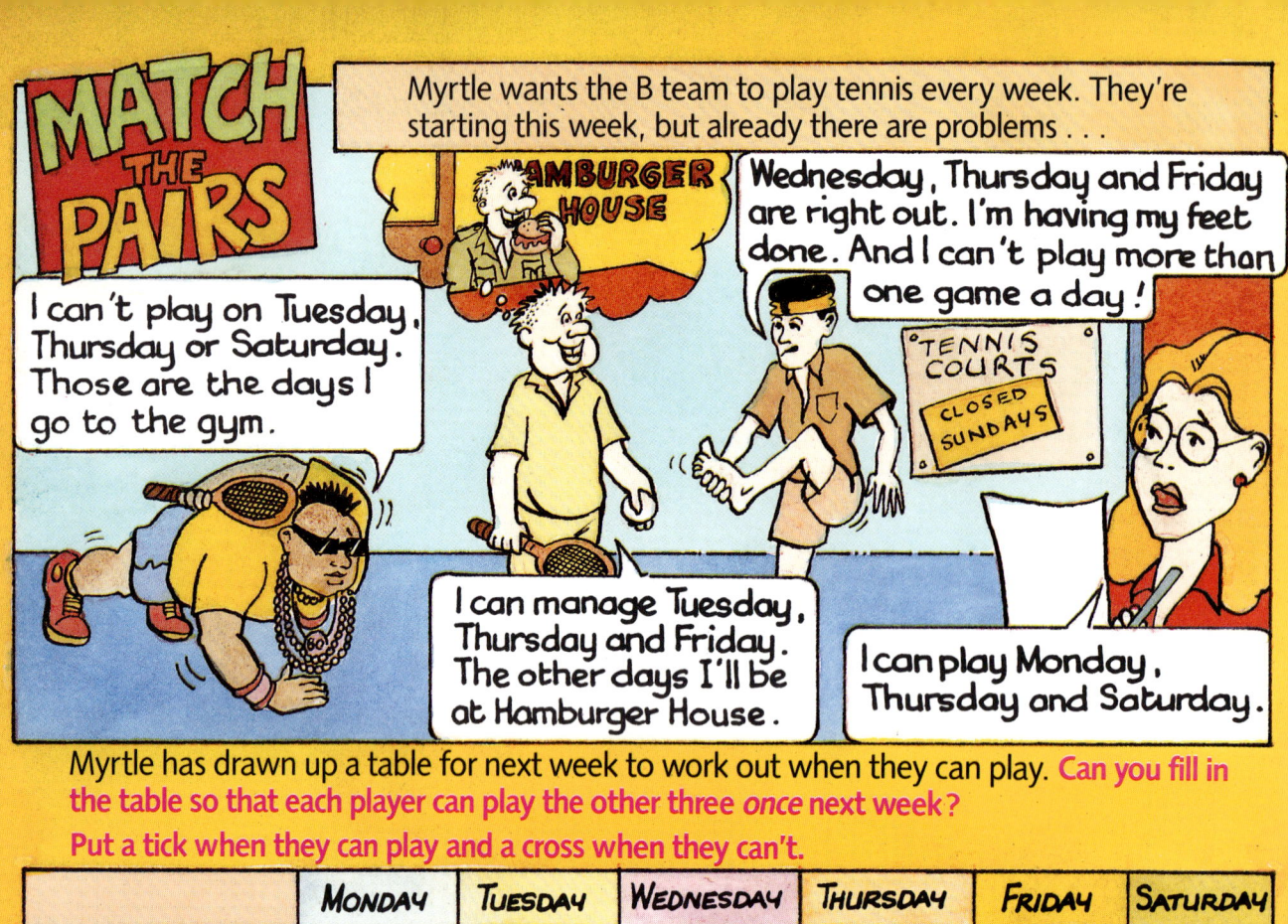

Myrtle wants the B team to play tennis every week. They're starting this week, but already there are problems...

Cannibal: I can't play on Tuesday, Thursday or Saturday. Those are the days I go to the gym.

Mr. U: I can manage Tuesday, Thursday and Friday. The other days I'll be at Hamburger House.

Feetman: Wednesday, Thursday and Friday are right out. I'm having my feet done. And I can't play more than one game a day!

Myrtle: I can play Monday, Thursday and Saturday.

TENNIS COURTS CLOSED SUNDAYS

Myrtle has drawn up a table for next week to work out when they can play. **Can you fill in the table so that each player can play the other three *once* next week?**

Put a tick when they can play and a cross when they can't.

	MONDAY	TUESDAY	WEDNESDAY	THURSDAY	FRIDAY	SATURDAY
MR. U						
CANNIBAL						
FEETMAN						
MYRTLE						

Is there any day when no game can be played (apart from Sunday)? —————

Is there a day when more than one game can be played? —————

MR. U   v .... ON ....
MR. U   v .... ON ....
MR. U   v .... ON ....
CANNIBAL   v .... ON ....
MYRTLE   v .... ON ....
MYRTLE   v .... ON ....

HIDDEN HEXAGONS

−6 −5 −4 −3 −2 −1 0 +1 +2 +3 +4 +5 +6 +7 +8 +9

Try it! Not all number lines start from 0. For example, some thermometers go below zero (0). If you count back from 0, you get −1, −2, −3, and so on. If you start at −5 (negative 5) and add 3, you get to −2 (negative 2).

Hidden hexagons is a game using negative numbers. Look at the red hexagon below. The six numbers inside it add up to 0.

This hexagon adds up to 0.

$^+4 + ^-7 + ^+2 + ^+5 + ^+1 + ^-5 = 0$

Can you find three more hidden hexagons which add up to 0? Use different coloured pencils to draw round each hexagon.

Why not make up hidden hexagons to try on your friends?

13

THE GREAT BUBBLE GUM Robbery

Gus's Grandad has planned the perfect robbery for Gus and Hatchet.

Grandad's Instructions

Walk from home to the bubble gum factory. Try not to look like burglars!

After the robbery, run to the school 3 kilometres from the bubble gum factory. I've hidden the tandem in the bike sheds.

Cycle to the Stolen Goods shop, taking the shortest route. But don't go past the police station.

I've booked you into a hotel, 5 kilometres from the Stolen Goods shop. It's very clean and quiet.

Here's the map. To avoid suspicion I haven't marked the route.

Sounds a nice little hotel, Gus.

Can you help Gus and Hatchet mark the route on the map?

How far is the whole journey, Hatch? Remember my Burglar's Bunions!

You need to use the scale to work out the distances.
The scale on the map is 2 cm = 1 km.
So 2 centimetres on the map means 1 kilometre.

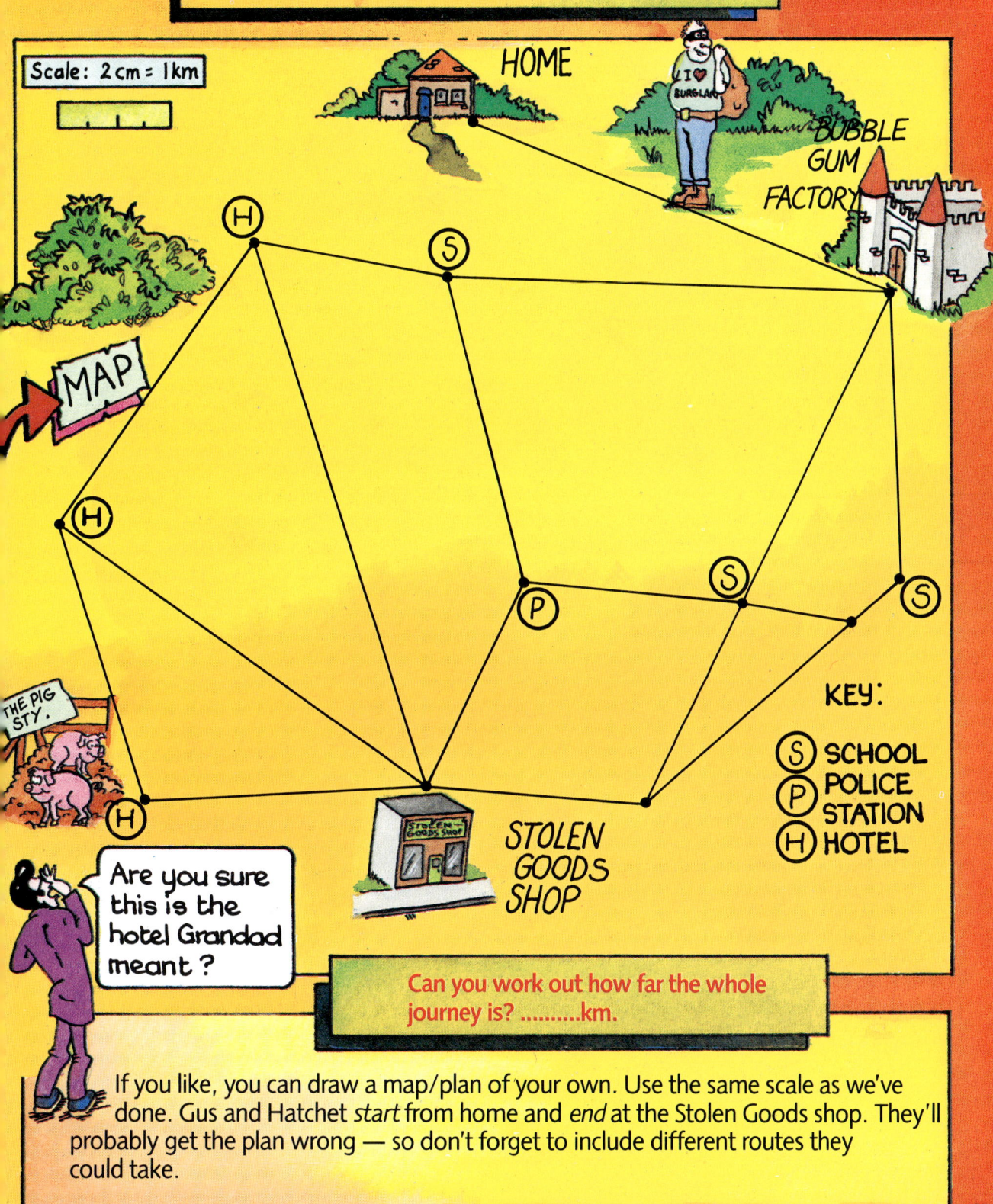

Scale: 2 cm = 1 km

HOME

BUBBLE GUM FACTORY

MAP

STOLEN GOODS SHOP

KEY:
(S) SCHOOL
(P) POLICE STATION
(H) HOTEL

THE PIG STY.

Are you sure this is the hotel Grandad meant?

Can you work out how far the whole journey is? .... km.

If you like, you can draw a map/plan of your own. Use the same scale as we've done. Gus and Hatchet *start* from home and *end* at the Stolen Goods shop. They'll probably get the plan wrong — so don't forget to include different routes they could take.

SPLODGE

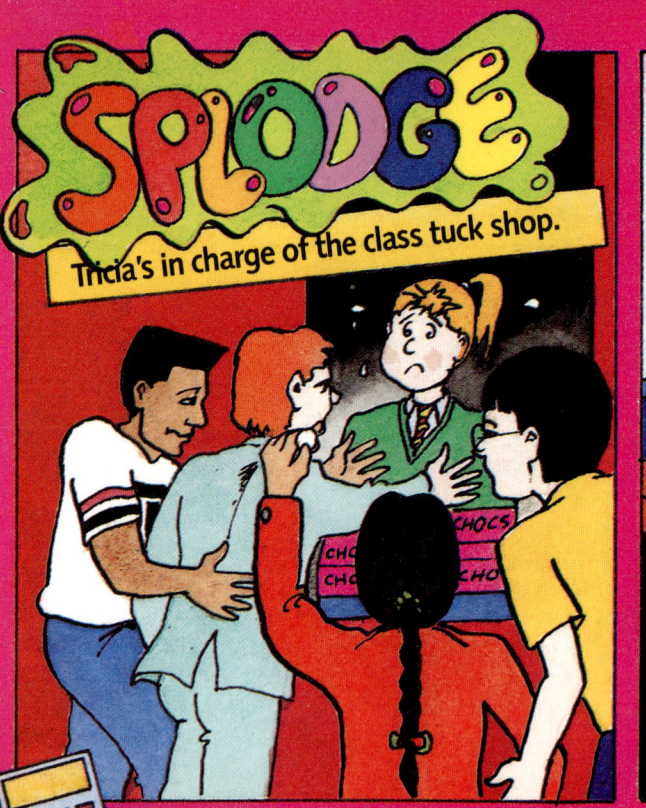

Tricia's in charge of the class tuck shop.

At the end of each day she works out how many of each item she has sold and counts up how much money she has taken.

Lisa makes a table for Tricia to work out her accounts. She helps Tricia by working out how much money they've made on each item. But some of her figures have got splodged.

Use your calculator to help you fill in the splodges. Do Tricia's totals for each day agree with Lisa's working out of how much they've made on each item?

ITEM	MONDAY	TUESDAY	WEDNESDAY	THURSDAY	FRIDAY
CRISPS (12p per packet)	14 PKTS = £1.68	19 PKTS = £3.99	25 PKTS =	15 PKTS = £1.80	12 PKTS = £1.44
CHOCOLATE BARS (16p per bar)	18 BARS = £2.88	13 BARS = £2.08	21 BARS = £3.36	19 BARS =	17 BARS =
FRUIT GUMS (11p per packet)	9 PKTS = 0.99	15 PKTS = £1.65	14 PKTS = £1.54	15 PKTS =	PKTS =
ORANGE JUICE (15p per carton)	33 CTNS =	29 CTNS = £4.35	37 CTNS =	31 CTNS =	25 CTNS = £3.75
APPLES (8p each)	11 APPLES = 0.88	8 APPLES = 0.64	10 APPLES =	11 APPLES =	13 APPLES =
TOTAL	£11.38	£11.00	£14.25	£12.02	£10.27

On Friday Tricia forgot to count the number of packets of fruit gums she sold. **Can you work it out for her?**

How much money did Tricia make in the whole week?

Total for week £ _____ .

16

"You've got it wrong!"

"No, you've got it wrong! You must have pressed a wrong button."

Which day are Tricia and Lisa arguing about? Look back at the chart. **Can you spot Lisa's mistake? Put ticks at the bottom for the right answers. Put a red circle round Lisa's mistake.**

Tricia sorts all the money into piles of coins to put them in bags to take to the bank.

She writes down the value of each bag, but some of her figures get splodged with fruit juice.

Can you fill them in for her?

	£1	50p	20p	10p	5p	2p	1p	TOTAL
NUMBER OF COINS	13	16		148		343	116	
VALUE	£13.00		£9.40	£14.80	£5.70		£1.16	£58.92

17

TAKING STOCK

The tuck shop has just run out of crisps.

No crisps in these boxes.

Idiot – you didn't order enough last week.

Paul decides to check how many packets of crisps and other items Tricia sold last week.

Just going back to page 16....

Look back at the chart on page 16 to find the missing numbers. **Can you complete this chart for Paul?** You'll need a calculator.

All right then, I'll order 6 million next week.

Item	Mon	Tues	Weds	Thurs	Fri	TOTAL
Packets of crisps	14	19	25	15	12	85
Choc bars	18	13	21	19	17	
Packets of fruit gums						
Cartons of orange juice						
Apples						

Trish, you need to buy more than you sell so you don't run out. We sold 85 packets of crisps last week, so we need 15 boxes of crisps this week.

The tuck shop buys its stock in boxes. The labels show how many items are in each b[ox]

CRISPS 6 PACKETS
CHOCOLATE BARS 24
ORANGE JUICE 12 SMALL CARTONS
FRUIT GUMS 48 PACKETS
36

How many *boxes* of the other items will they need? Remember to round up the totals to the nearest box.

CHOC BARS	
FRUIT GUMS	
ORANGE JUICE	
APPLES	

Pentominoes

A domino has 2 squares. You can only make 1 shape with 2 squares.

A triomino has 3 squares. You can only make 2 shapes with 3 squares.

A quadromino has 4 squares. You can make 5 shapes with 4 squares.

A pentomino has 5 squares. Here are 3 shapes you can make with 5 squares.

How many more pentomino shapes can you make with 5 squares? All the pentomino shapes are hidden in this rectangle. We've coloured in 6 of them.
How many more can you find?

Use different colours to shade them in. There should be no squares left over.

Pentominoes

There are 12 pentominoes. **Did you find them all?**

You can use the rectangle below to make a shape jigsaw. On a piece of stiff paper draw a rectangle the same size as the one below. Draw in the 12 pentomino shapes. Cut carefully round each one.

How many different ways can you find of fitting your 12 pentomino shapes on to the rectangle? Ask your friends to try it!

QUEEN of HEARTS

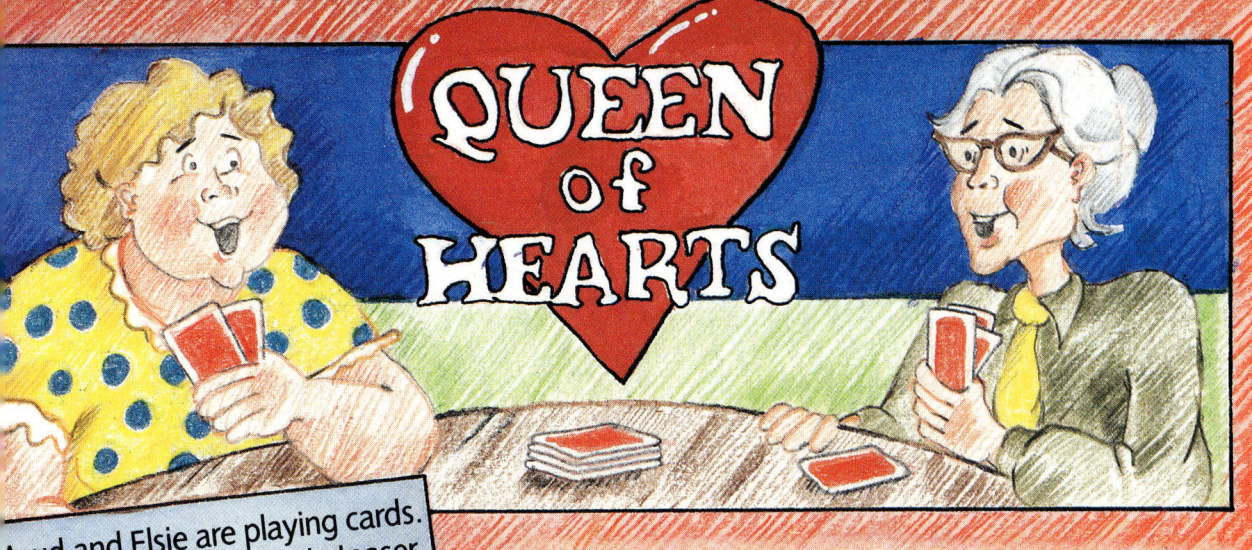

Maud and Elsie are playing cards. Maud has set Elsie a brain teaser.

Take out the following cards from the pack: all the picture cards — Kings, Queens and Jacks — and all the Aces.

SET 7 OF THE CARDS OUT LIKE THIS:

Your aim is to make 4 rows of 4 cards.

Each row must have an Ace, King, Queen and Jack.
Each column must have an Ace, King, Queen and Jack.
Both diagonals must have an Ace, King, Queen and Jack.

Each row must have one of each suit.
Each column must have one of each suit.
Both diagonals must have one of each suit.

CAN YOU DO IT?

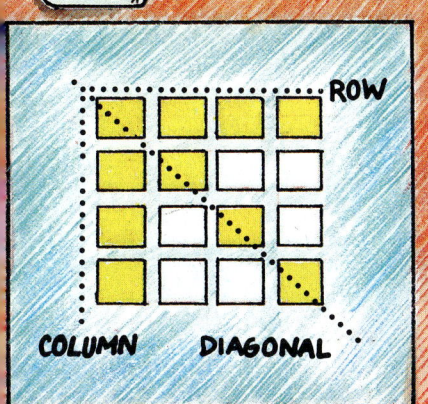

Don't forget, Elsie, you can only have *one* of the same face and *one* of the same suit in any row, column or diagonal.

ROW
COLUMN   DIAGONAL

COOKING WITH SKULK

1.

DOWN WITH LICE AND WORM PIE

SLUG SANDWICHES ARE BORING!!

RECIPE BOOK

We need something new on the menu. Our customers are revolting!

2. There's a recipe here for Iced Sultana Buns.

Sultanas! Yuk! How disgusting.

Here is the recipe, for 16 buns. Weigh the ingredients carefully.

Can you make Iced Sultana Buns for Skulk and Gargoyle's Guest House? First ask an adult whether you may use the oven.

3.

100 g (4 oz) self raising flour
100 g (4 oz) caster sugar
50 g (2 oz) soft margarine
75 g (3 oz) sultanas
25 ml (1 fl oz) milk
2 eggs
a pinch of salt

1. Heat the oven to Gas Mark 5, or 375°F (190°C) if using electricity.
2. First beat the margarine and sugar together in a bowl, using a wooden spoon (or a hand mixer on slow speed); then add the beaten eggs.
3. Mix in the flour and salt; add the milk and mix everything together until smooth.
4. Mix in the sultanas.
5. Spoon into 16 paper cases.
6. Bake in the oven for 15-20 minutes until the sponge is firm but springy.

While the buns are cooling make the Chocolate Butter Icing:

200 g (8 oz) sieved icing sugar
40 g (1½ oz) butter or margarine
2 teaspoons cocoa powder
1 teaspoon vanilla essence

1. Soften the butter or margarine and beat in the icing sugar.
2. Add a few teaspoons of water until the icing is soft, but not runny.
3. Add the cocoa powder and mix into the icing.
4. Spread the icing on the buns.

4

"They love them....! We'd better make some more. Make twice as many this time."

Work out the quantities Skulk and Gargoyle will need to make 32 buns. Write the recipe for 32 Iced Sultana Buns for Skulk's Recipe Book.

Skulk's favourite recipes

Iced Sultana Buns (makes 32)

Ingredients

- ☐ ( ) self raising flour
- ☐ ( ) caster sugar
- ☐ ( ) soft margarine
- ☐ ( ) sultanas
- ☐ ( ) milk
- ☐ eggs
- ☐ pinches of salt

Chocolate Butter Icing

- ☐ ( ) sieved icing sugar
- ☐ ( ) butter or margarine
- ☐ teaspoons cocoa powder
- ☐ teaspoons vanilla essence

Weedy's Calculator Games

Bet I can find out how old you are, Dad!

Weedy tries this game out on his Dad.

GAME 1 — Ages and ages

Here is a way of getting someone to tell you their age without them knowing it. Give them a calculator and ask them secretly to enter the number of the month they were born in (January = 1, February = 2, and so on).

Then ask them to:
1. multiply the number by 5
2. add 42
3. multiply by 20
4. add their age in years
5. subtract 840

If you look at the result, the last 2 digits give their age in years, while the first digit(s) show the month.

You can check this works by trying it out yourself.
You can try it again with these numbers:
- add 32 instead of 42 and finish by subtracting 640 instead of 840.

See if you can work out how it's done.

Hey, Dad, you're 140!

Stupid, Weedy, you pressed the wrong key!

GAME 2 — Keep the change!
(A calculator game for 2 players)

You have £10 to spend on fireworks.
Your partner chooses the price of each firework.
You must decide, without hesitating, how many you want to buy.

However... whatever you don't spend, your partner gets to keep.
And if you spend more than the £10 your partner gets the lot!

The winner is the player with the most money after 5 goes each.

	Weedy	Tricia
1	£3.55	£____
2		
3		
4		
5		

You go first, Trish. I say the price of each firework is £2·15.

I'll buy, um, 3.

Ha, ha! You've only spent £6·45. That's £3·55 to me — very generous of you, Trish.

Okay, Greedy Weedy, my turn. I'll give you a price of 78 pence for each Firework.

Right, then I'll buy 13.

As you get sneakier at this game, you may have to change the rules a bit!

How much did Tricia win?
£...........

If you liked these calculator games, try this one. It's a bit more difficult.

GAME 3
Times and times again

1. Enter any number up to 100 into the calculator.
2. Multiply by another number, so that the result is a number which starts with 1.
3. See if you can multiply this result by another number so that the answer starts with 2.
4. Now keep multiplying and see if you can get numbers which start with 3, 4 and 5.

You could play this game with a friend.
Write the answers down.
If you get it right first time, score 2 points.
If you get it right second time, score 1 point.
If you can't get it right third time, you're out.
The winner is the person with the most points.

1,   53
2, (×3=) 159
3, (×18=) 2862
4, (×12=) 34344

This is what Sid did.

So am I!

I'm tired....

Gus and Hatchet's

STOLEN GOODS

"What's 10%, Hatch?"

"Look, Gus, £7 is the full price. That's 100%. 10% off means you pay 90% of the full price. That's 90% of £7."

You'll need a calculator to work out percentages. Has your calculator got a percentage key on it, like this?

Hatchet's has. This is how he worked out *10% off £7*:

FIRST TAKE AWAY 10 FROM 100, THEN:

7 × 9 0 % = 6:30

TWO DAYS LATER

Can you work out all the sale prices in Gus and Hatchet's Super Sale? Fill in all the new prices on the price tags. One has already been done for you.

SET OF 3 WAS £9.50 30% OFF. NEW PRICE:

WAS £1.25 20% OFF. NEW PRICE:

WAS £7.50 50% OFF. NEW PRICE:

WAS £7 10% OFF. NEW PRICE: £6.30

VISA ACCESS

DISCOUNT SALE!

"What about 25% off, Hatch?"

"A percentage is an easy way of working out part of something. The percentage line will help you to understand how it works."

Can you work out 25% *off* £7 on your calculator and fill in the answer?

FIRST TAKE AWAY 25 FROM 100, THEN:

| 7 | × | 7 5 | % | = | |

WAS £20
30% OFF.
NEW PRICE:

FAMOUS PAINTING
WAS £25
25% OFF.
NEW PRICE:

WAS £3.80
50% OFF.
NEW PRICE:

WAS £3.50
10% OFF.
NEW PRICE:

WAS £8.80
25% OFF.
NEW PRICE:

WAS £7.50
20% OFF.
NEW PRICE:

THE DARTS COMPETITION

Maud and Elsie have joined their local darts team. They play with 4 other friends — Jean, Dorcas, Violet and Kath. They meet at the Women's Centre twice a week. They want to get in a lot of practice before they play a real match

Maud has decided that they should *all play each other once*. She has written a chart for the club notice board. The first game will be between Maud and Elsie.

Can you finish this chart for Maud? Write the names in the first 4 boxes. Draw the other boxes on the chart and fill in all the names.

NOTICE BOARD

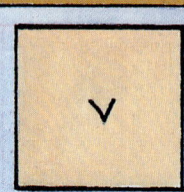

| MAUD v ELSIE | MAUD v | v | v |

How many games will be played altogether?   How many times will they each play?

Maud and Elsie are in the last round of their game. The winner is the first one to reach 200.

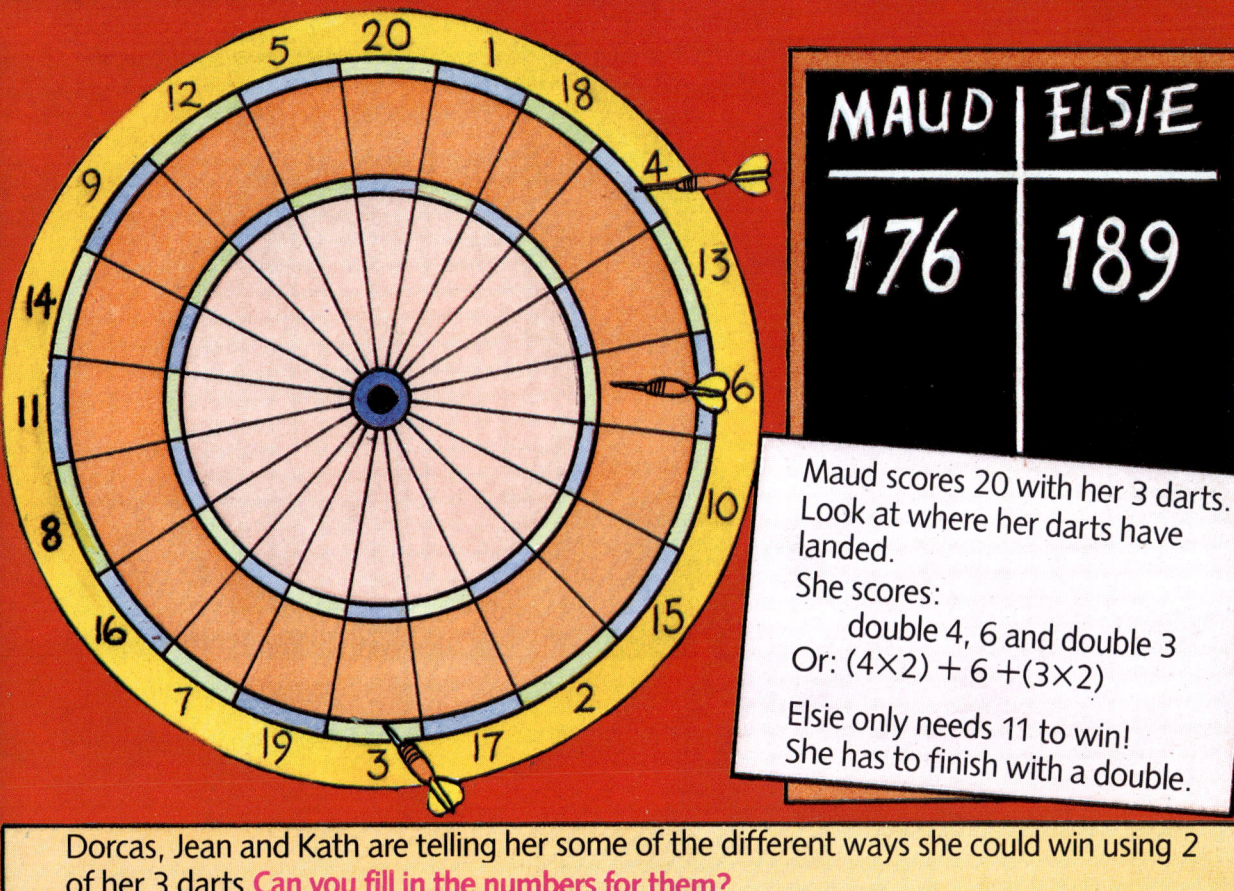

MAUD	ELSIE
176	189

Maud scores 20 with her 3 darts. Look at where her darts have landed.
She scores:
　　double 4, 6 and double 3
Or: (4×2) + 6 +(3×2)

Elsie only needs 11 to win! She has to finish with a double.

Dorcas, Jean and Kath are telling her some of the different ways she could win using 2 of her 3 darts. **Can you fill in the numbers for them?**

Come on Elsie! You can do it. ☐ and double ☐ !

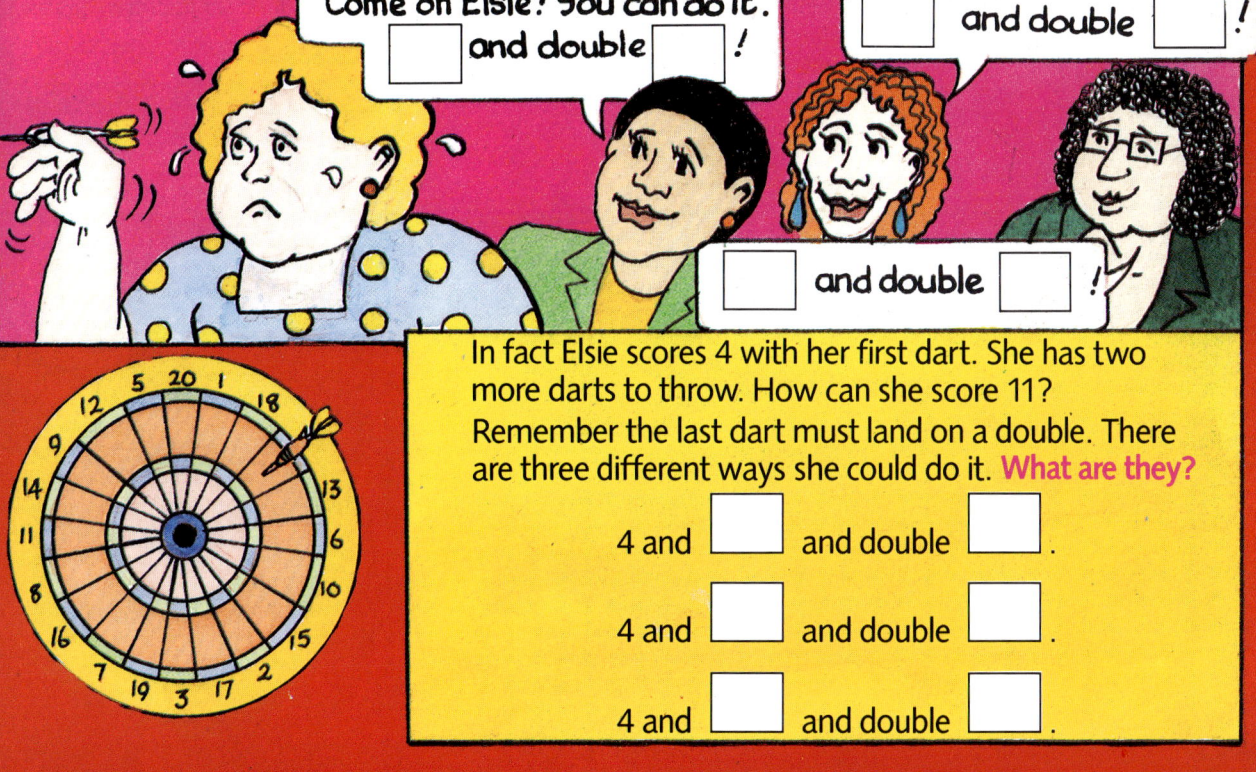

☐ and double ☐ !

☐ and double ☐ !

In fact Elsie scores 4 with her first dart. She has two more darts to throw. How can she score 11? Remember the last dart must land on a double. There are three different ways she could do it. **What are they?**

4 and ☐ and double ☐ .

4 and ☐ and double ☐ .

4 and ☐ and double ☐ .

THE 100 METRES SPRINT

Carl Lewis from the United States and Canada's Ben Johnson have battled for the 100 metres since they first raced each other in 1980.

Here are their timings *in seconds* from the most important races.

100 metres sprint	Carl Lewis	Ben Johnson
1980 Pan American Games	10.43	10.88
1984 Olympic Games	9.99	10.22
1987, Seville, Spain	10.05	10.04
1987, Rome 2nd World Championships	9.93	9.83

- When did Lewis first beat Johnson? ....
- When did Johnson first beat Lewis? ....
- Which was their closest race? ....
- Who has the fastest time of all? ....

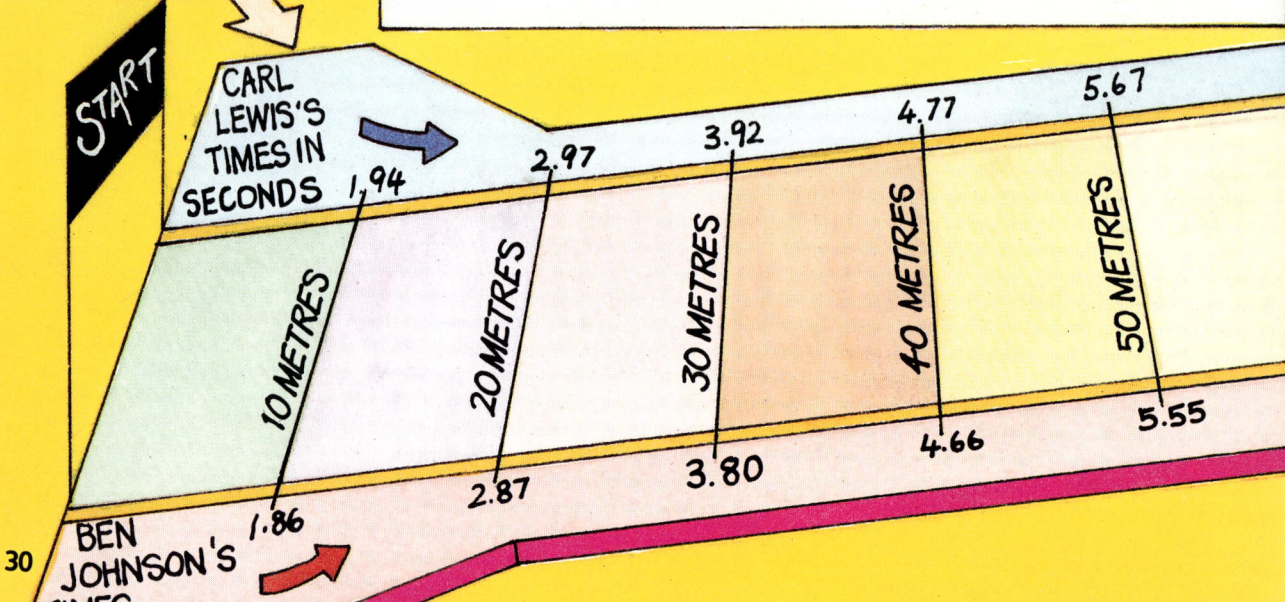

Here are the times that Johnson and Lewis took to reach each 10 metre mark:

START

CARL LEWIS'S TIMES IN SECONDS
- 10 METRES: 1.94
- 20 METRES: 2.97
- 30 METRES: 3.92
- 40 METRES: 4.77
- 50 METRES: 5.67

BEN JOHNSON'S TIMES IN SECONDS
- 10 METRES: 1.86
- 20 METRES: 2.87
- 30 METRES: 3.80
- 40 METRES: 4.66
- 50 METRES: 5.55

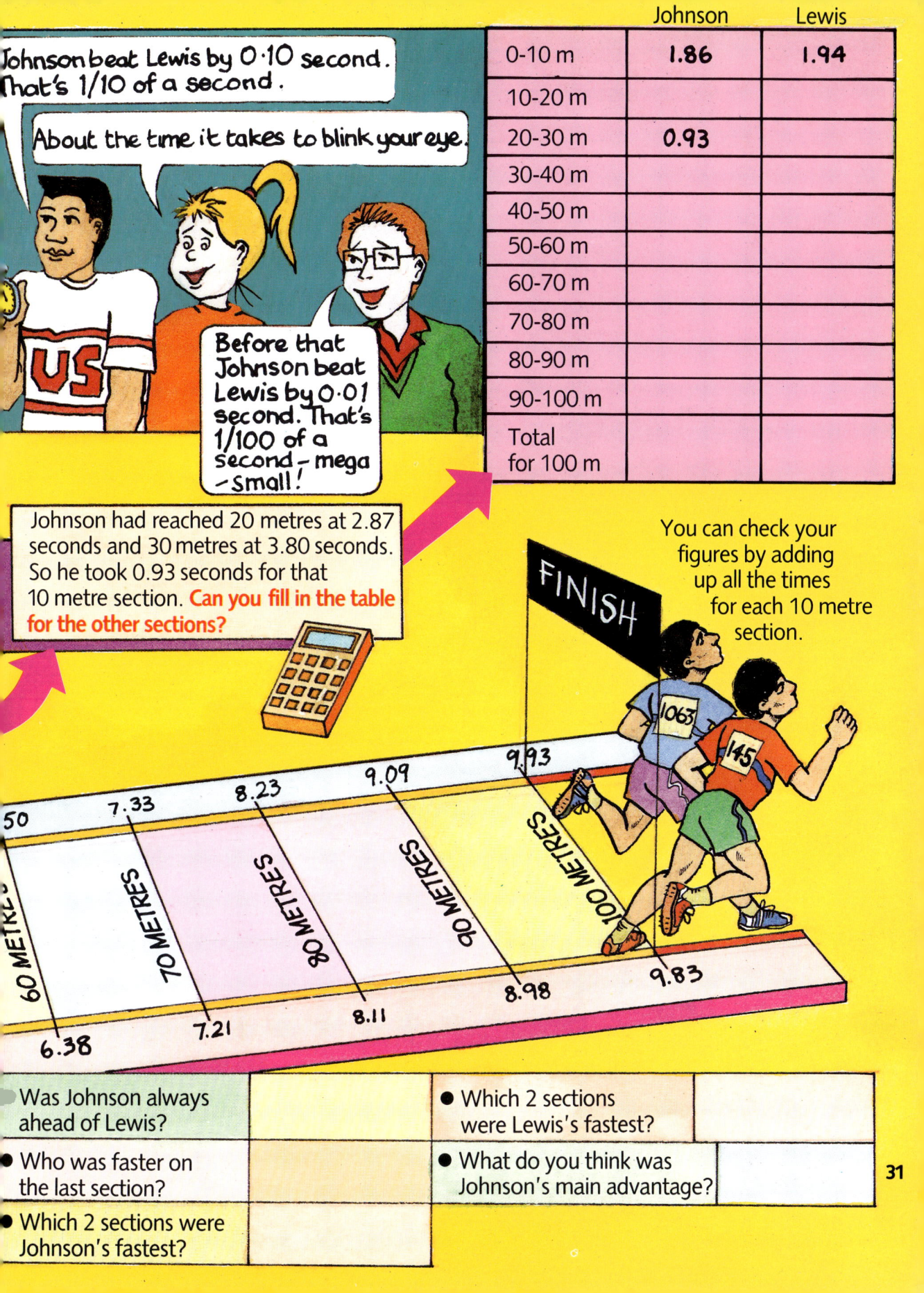

"Johnson beat Lewis by 0.10 second. That's 1/10 of a second."

"About the time it takes to blink your eye."

"Before that Johnson beat Lewis by 0.01 second. That's 1/100 of a second – mega-small!"

	Johnson	Lewis
0-10 m	1.86	1.94
10-20 m		
20-30 m	0.93	
30-40 m		
40-50 m		
50-60 m		
60-70 m		
70-80 m		
80-90 m		
90-100 m		
Total for 100 m		

Johnson had reached 20 metres at 2.87 seconds and 30 metres at 3.80 seconds. So he took 0.93 seconds for that 10 metre section. **Can you fill in the table for the other sections?**

You can check your figures by adding up all the times for each 10 metre section.

Track markings:
- 50 / 6.38
- 60 METRES
- 70 METRES / 7.33 / 7.21
- 80 METRES / 8.23 / 8.11
- 90 METRES / 9.09 / 8.98
- 100 METRES / 9.93 / 9.83

- Was Johnson always ahead of Lewis?
- Who was faster on the last section?
- Which 2 sections were Johnson's fastest?
- Which 2 sections were Lewis's fastest?
- What do you think was Johnson's main advantage?

WHO WATCHES MOST TELEVISION?

1 Hey, you lot! Did you know that, on average, people watch 25 hours of television a week?

2 Bet you watch more than the average!

Bet I don't.

3 Don't forget there are 60 minutes in an hour. So add up carefully!

TRICIA

DAY:	PROGRAMME:	LENGTH: HR:	MIN:
Monday	Children's ITV	1	15
	Neighbours		25
Tuesday	Neighbours		25
	Eastenders		30
	Anne of Green Gables	1	15
Wednesday	Neighbours		25
	Figure skating	1	
Thursday	Children's ITV	1	15
	Neighbours		25
	Eastenders		30
Friday	Neighbours		25
	Chart show		30
	6 O'clock Show	1	
Saturday	Wide Awake Club	1	55
	Saturday afternoon film	2	
	Blockbusters		30
	A team		25
Sunday	Old black and white film	1	50
	Adventures of Black Beauty		30
	Agatha Christie	1	
	TOTAL HOURS' VIEWING		

Sid and Tricia wrote down all the programmes Tricia watched in one week. They wrote down the length of time each programme lasted. **Can you add up the total for the week?**

The children worked out how much TV the 4 of them watched every day. They added up the totals for one week. Then they divided each total by 7 to work out their daily average.

When you add up the total for the week, you can round the minutes up or down to the nearest 15 minutes.

MINUTES	FRACTIONS	DECIMALS
15	¼	0·25
30	½	0·5
45	¾	0·75

Hey, how do you divide 26 hours and 15 minutes by 7 on a calculator?

Your calculator uses decimal points, not minutes. So you need to change the minutes to decimal fractions. Here's a handy hint to help you.

This is what the 4 of them wrote. **Can you work out each of their daily averages?**

If you turn over there's a chart *you* can fill in!

Bet no-one in the whole world watches as much TV as Weedy.

	HOURS PER WEEK	DAILY AVERAGE
TRICIA		
SID	7	
LISA	12.25	
WEEDY	26.25	

WHAT'S YOUR AVERAGE?

Can you fill in this chart with all the programmes you watch in one week? If you're not sure how long a programme lasts, check a newspaper or the Radio Times and TV Times.

Day	Programme	Length	
		hr	min

TOTAL HOURS' VIEWING

Personalised! You can write your name here.

Hey, this looks like work. There's something I must *watch on TV.*

Did you see the Denver Broncos live on Sunday night? Wicked.

That's disgusting! It goes on until after midnight.

Do you watch more or less television than the average?

If you like, you can get together with some friends to work out your average *daily* viewing.

34

STAMPS!

Ghoul End Post Office has a new book of stamps that costs 31p. There are 5 stamps in the book.
The 'teaser' is that these 5 stamps make up every value from 1p to 31p.

Here are the five stamps. But none of the prices have been written in.

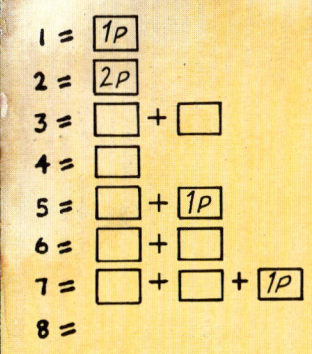

☐p ☐p ☐p ☐p ☐p

Can you work out what stamp prices are needed to complete the table?
REMEMBER: You can only use each stamp once to make up each value.
We've made a start for you.

1 = [1p]
2 = [2p]
3 = ☐ + ☐
4 = ☐
5 = ☐ + [1p]
6 = ☐ + ☐
7 = ☐ + ☐ + [1p]
8 =
9 =
10 =
11 =
12 =
13 =
14 =
15 =
16 =
17 =
18 =
19 =
20 =
21 =
22 =
23 =
24 =
25 =
26 =
27 =
28 =
29 =
30 =
31 =

What 5 stamps did you need?

Can you now fill in the prices on the stamps above?

Costing the Ghouls' Holiday

A family of 4 ghouls — 2 grown ups and 2 young ones — and their pet werewolf want to go on a 14 day holiday. They only have £600 to spend for all their rooms and meals. They want 2 double rooms, and 3 meals a day. They'd like to go at the most popular time of year (November) if they can afford it.

GARGOYLE'S GUEST HOUSE

BED AND BREAKFAST

Double room, 1 week £60
Dinner, each evening ...... £3·50 per ghoul
No Lunches, but we do packed midnight snacks, for ghoul outings. (for 4 ghouls) .... £4·50

Daily guided tours of Skulk's Sluggery
Delightful rooms - damp, dirty and cold
Special food for pet werewolves .... £1 per day

Full board means room and all meals. Half board means room, breakfast and evening meal only.

Ghoul Gables

HALF BOARD

Charge per night
for a double room £15

Lunches, if required .... £2.50 per ghoul

Extra charge in November
Grown ups .... £10 per week
Young ones .... £15 per week

FREE OF CHARGE!
Mud baths
Running water in all rooms
Use of cesspool

Mouldy mattresses extra

Bonecrusher's Beautiful Bungalow

FULL BOARD

Double room – 1 week   £180
– 2 weeks   £340

ALL ROOMS WITH VIEW:
Sea view – £30 off full weekly price
Cemetery view – £40 extra a week

Lovely beach only a slug's throw from the hotel – guaranteed pure white quicksand
Shark infested sea

Rooms must be vacated by midnight.

Pet werewolves welcome – FREE
(But please don't let them howl during the day.)

Which of the hotels can the ghoul family afford?

....
....

You'll need a calculator, pencil and paper to work out the different costs:

- how many rooms will they need?
- when do they need to spend extra on meals?
- what other extra charges are there?

Imagine the ghouls want to go to Velda Vampire's Leisure Centre every day of their holiday. They have £50 to spend for all the family. Can you make up a programme showing all the sports and games available, and how much each costs?

SMASH HIT?

The B-Team aren't happy about the sales of their latest album.

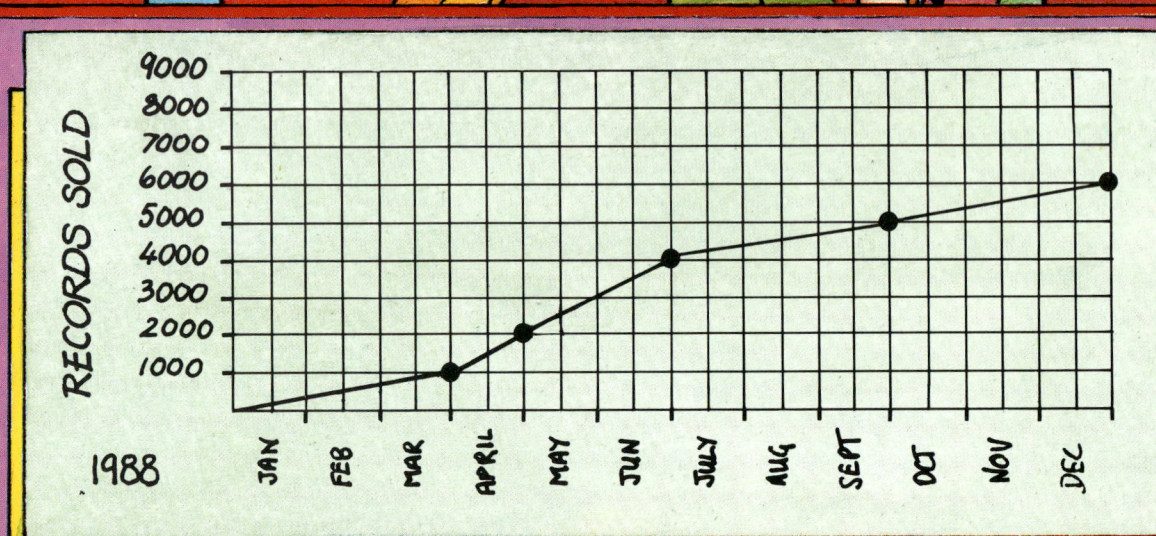

- How many records did they sell in 1988? ....
- How many records did they sell in the first three months of 1988? ....
- In which three months did they sell the most records? ....

One year later...

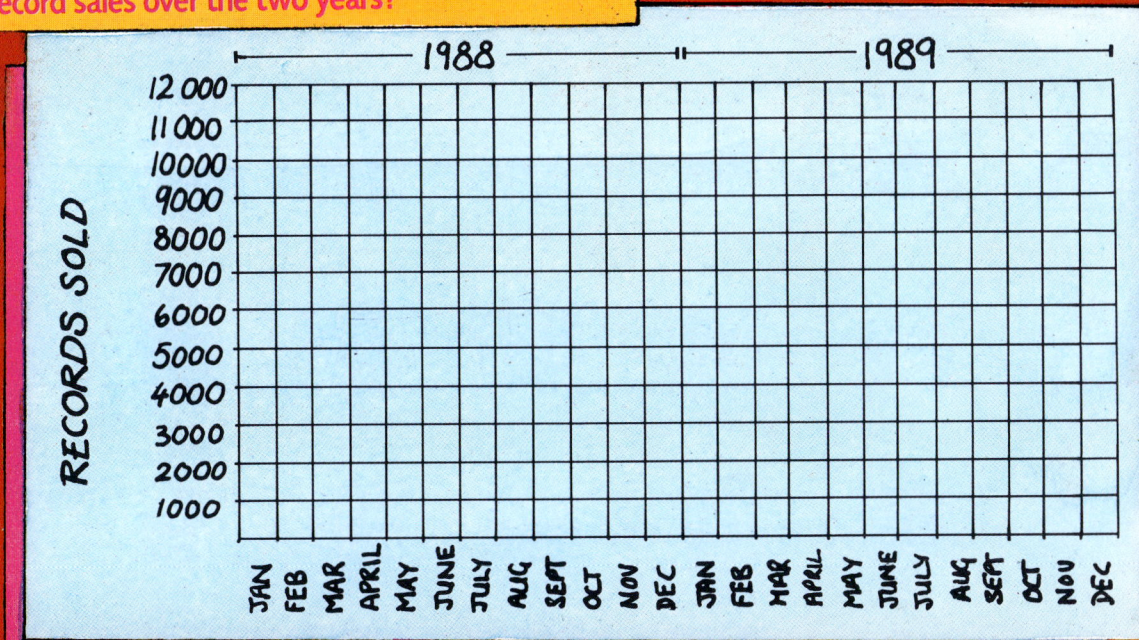

See.... I told you things would look better this year.

Then why aren't we getting more money?

- How many records did they sell in 1989? ....
- Did they sell more or less records in 1989 than in 1988? ....
- The group had a big concert in 1989. This helped them sell more records in one month than in any other month in 1989. Which month was it? ....

The new manager has done something to make sales look better. **Can you see what it is?**

Can you fill in this graph to give a true picture of the record sales over the two years?

MOVING DAY for tatty tricia

Before you look at this page, read page 41 and then cut it out.

Tricia's got a problem. She can't fit all the furniture in her new bedroom.

So Tricia and Sid decided to make a plan of the bedroom to find out what will fit in.

Tricia measured the room, including all the things she couldn't move around, like the window and the door. Sid wrote down all the measurements.

Sid decided that the scale should be 20:1. Tricia's window measured 180 centimetres (the same as 1.8 metres). So Sid *divided* the *real* 180 cm by 20 to get the *scale* measurement of 9 cm.

Then he drew a plan of Tricia's bedroom. Look at the plan on page 43.

After that Sid measured all the things you could move around. Tricia wrote down all the measurements. Then she drew a scale drawing of each one. **Look at the scale drawings on page 41.**

There are 10 pieces of furniture. 5 pieces must go in. These are the ones with red letters. The 5 pieces with blue letters are not so important. Tricia says she must have 3 of them in her room, but it doesn't matter which 3.

Cut out the whole of this page. Now cut out the scale drawings of Tricia's furniture.

If you make any mistakes in cutting out, you can make your own scale drawing. Use the scale measurements on the back.

Scale: 20:1

Bedside table

Wardrobe

Desk

Bed

Games cupboard

Dressing table

Chest

Dolls' house

Bookcase

Chair

Can you work out what the real measurements are? Multiply each measurement here by 20. You'll need your calculator. If you like, you can write the *real* measurements next to the *scale* measurements.

You can look at things in your own bedroom when you're moving these drawings around.

SCALE = 20:1

BED — 10 cm × 5 cm

BEDSIDE TABLE — 2.5 cm × 2.5 cm

DESK — 6 cm × 3.5 cm

WARDROBE — 5 cm × 2.5 cm

GAMES CUPBOARD — 4 cm × 3 cm

DRESSING TABLE — 5 cm × 2.5 cm

CHEST — 5 cm × 2.5 cm

DOLLS' HOUSE — 4 cm × 4 cm

CHAIR — 2 cm × 2 cm

BOOKCASE — 6 cm × 1.5 cm

42

Move the drawings around on the plan. What's the best way to arrange all the furniture?

Which 2 pieces of furniture did you leave out? .... and .... Can you make a plan like this for your own bedroom?

Can you help Tricia think about these things?

- enough space to move around the room?
- what do I want to use the room for?
- what things can't go in front of the window?
- what would be nice in front of the window?
- what do I want near the sockets?

SOCKET

WALL 16 cm (320 cm)

WALL 18 cm (360 cm)

WINDOW 9 cm (180 cm)

DOOR 4.5 cm (90 cm)

SOCKET

Scale = 20:1

MOTORWAY "MADNESS"

The B-mobile has broken down again.

It's Cannibal's fault. We've run out of petrol again!

WHAT MYRTLE SEES!

If Myrtle drives at roughly 45 mph all the way, the van will do 25 miles on 5 litres of petrol. But if Cannibal drives at 75 mph, it only does 15 miles on 5 litres.

It's because you drive too fast.

The way I drive, there shouldn't be time to run out of petrol!

We've got a case in Blueville on Saturday. That's 225 miles. We can't afford to run out of petrol again.

Myrtle works out the amount of petrol.

MYRTLE DRIVING	CANNIBAL DRIVING
25 MILES USES 5 LITRES 225 MILES USES ....LITRES	15 MILES USES 5 LITRES 225 MILES USES ....LITRES

Mr U. works out how long the journey will take

MYRTLE DRIVING	CANNIBAL DRIVING
SPEED = 45 MPH DISTANCE = 225 MILES JOURNEY TIME = ...HOURS	SPEED = 75 MPH DISTANCE = 225 MILES JOURNEY TIME = ...HOURS

Can you finish the calculations for them? You'll need a calculator.

Myrtle agrees to share the driving with Cannibal.

Here are the distances between each town they will drive past.
Can you fill in the distances between Holly Springs and Blueville?

HOME TO CONCORDIA	CONCORDIA TO HOLLY SPRINGS	HOLLY SPRINGS TO BLUEVILLE
45 MILES	75 MILES	_____ MILES

HOME   BLUEVILLE

Can you complete this simple map of their journey? It's drawn to scale: 1 cm = 15 miles. Where should Concordia and Holly Springs go?

Cannibal will drive to Holly Springs. Myrtle will drive from Holly Springs to Blueville.

Can you work out how much petrol they will use on each stage of the journey? .... and .... litres

How much will they use altogether? .... litres

How long will the whole journey take? .... hours
(Round your answer up to the nearest hour.)

On Saturday . . .

"Who forgot to check the tyres.....?!"

45

ANSWER PAGE

Page 8
Amazing millions!
A million £1 coins weigh 9.3 tonnes
Peking
A million babies are born in just under 12 days
There are a million extra people in the world in 4 days, 15 hours, 6 minutes, 40 seconds.

Page 10
Too many to count
On one page of Weedy's telephone book there are 360 Smiths.
On 8 pages there are 2880 Smiths.
Sid and Weedy estimated 5616 cars for the whole day.

Page 12
Match the pairs
Mr U v Feetman on Monday
Mr U v Myrtle on Monday
Mr U v Cannibal on Friday
Cannibal v Feetman on Tuesday
Myrtle v Cannibal on Thursday
Myrtle v Feetman on Saturday
No game can be played on Wednesday
Two games can be played on Monday

Page 13
Hidden hexagons

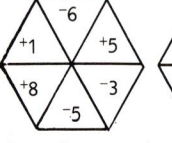

Page 14
The great bubble gum robbery
The whole journey is 16 km.

Page 16
Splodge
Crisps on Wednesday	25 pkts = £3
Chocolate bars on Thursday	19 bars = £3.04
on Friday	17 bars = £2.72
Fruit gums on Thursday	15 pkts = £1.65
on Friday	12 pkts = £1.32
Orange juice on Monday	33 ctns = £4.95
on Wednesday	37 ctns = £5.55
on Thursday	31 ctns = £4.65
Apples on Wednesday	10 apples = £0.80
on Thursday	11 apples = £0.88
on Friday	13 apples = £1.04

On Friday Tricia sold 12 packets of fruit gums.
Total for week £58.92.

Lisa's mistake was on Tuesday. 19 packets of crisps at 12p per packet cost £2.28

Tricia's table
	£1	50p	20p	10p	5p	2p	1p	TOTAL
No. of coins	13	16	47	148	114	343	116	797
Value	£13	£8	£9.40	£14.80	£5.70	£6.86	£1.16	£58.92

Page 18
Taking stock
Item	Mon	Tues	Wed	Thurs	Fri	TOTAL
Packets of crisps	14	19	25	15	12	85
Choc bars	18	13	21	19	17	88
Packets of fruit gums	9	15	14	15	12	65
Cartons of orange juice	33	29	37	31	25	155
Apples	11	8	10	11	13	53

Choc bars	4
Fruit gums	2
Orange juice	13
Apples	2

Page 21
Queen of Hearts
Here is one solution; see if you can find others.

Page 22
Cooking with Skulk
Iced sultana buns (makes 32)
200 g (8 oz) self raising flour
200 g (8 oz) caster sugar
100 g (4 oz) soft margarine
150 g (6 oz) sultanas
50 ml (2 fl oz) milk
4 eggs
2 pinches of salt
Chocolate butter icing
400 g (16 oz) sieved icing sugar
80 g (3 oz) butter or margarine
4 teaspoons cocoa powder
2 teaspoons vanilla essence

Page 24
Weedy's calculator games
Tricia won £10.14.

Page 26
Gus and Hatchet's discount sale!
25% off £7 = £5.25

Garden gnomes: new price £6.65
Television set: new price £14
Painting: new price £18.75
Dead plant: new price £1.90
Bike: new price £6
Clock: new price £1
Ladder: new price £3.75
Wheelbarrow: new price £6.60
Lavatory seat: new price £3.15

Page 28
The darts competition
Maud v Elsie   Maud v Violet   Violet v Kath   Kath v Jean
Violet v Dorcas   Jean v Dorcas   Dorcas v Elsie   Elsie v Violet
Violet v Jean   Jean v Maud   Dorcas v Kath   Kath v Maud
Maud v Dorcas   Elsie v Jean   Elsie v Kath

Altogether they play 15 games. They each play 5 times.

Elsie could throw 1 and double 5	7 and double 2	After she throws 4	1 and double 3
3 and double 4	9 and double 1	she could throw:	or 3 and double 2
5 and double 3			or 5 and double 1

Page 30
The 100 metres sprint
	JOHNSON	LEWIS
0-10m	1.86	1.94
10-20	1.01	1.03
20-30	0.93	0.95
30-40	0.86	0.85
40-50	0.89	0.90
50-60	0.83	0.83
60-70	0.83	0.83
70-80	0.90	0.90
80-90	0.87	0.86
90-100	0.85	0.84
TOTAL	9.83	9.93

Johnson was always ahead of Lewis.
Lewis was faster on the last section.
Johnson's fastest sections were 50-60m and 60-70m.
Lewis's fastest sections were 50-60m and 60-70m.
Johnson's main advantage was a fast start.

Page 32
Who watches most television?
Tricia: total hours' viewing 17.5 hours

Daily average:
Tricia   2.5 hours (or 2 hours 30 minutes)
Sid   1 hour
Lisa   1.75 hours (or 1 hour 45 minutes)
Weedy   3.75 hours (or 3 hours 45 minutes)

Page 35
Stamps!
The five stamps are 1p, 2p, 4p, 8p, 16p.

Page 36
Costing the ghouls' holiday
The costs are:
Gargoyle's Guest House   £513
Ghoul Gables   £660
Bonecrusher's Bungalow
  2 rooms with sea view   £560
  2 rooms with cemetery view   £840

So they can afford Gargoyle's Guest House and Bonecrusher's Beautiful Bungalow if they take 2 rooms with sea view.

Page 38
Smash hit?
The B team sold 6000 records in 1988.
They sold 1000 in the first three months.
They sold most records between March and June 1988: 3000
In 1989 they sold 5000 records — 1000 less than in 1988.
Their big concert was in October.
The manager altered the scale of the graph to make it look better.

Page 44
Motorway madness
Myrtle driving
225 miles uses 45 litres
Journey time — 5 hours

Cannibal driving
225 miles uses 75 litres
Journey time — 3 hours

Holly Springs to Blueville — 105 miles
They use 40 and 21 litres — 61 litres altogether
They will take 4 hours (rounded up to the nearest hour)

46

the SUCCESS! AWARDS CEREMONY

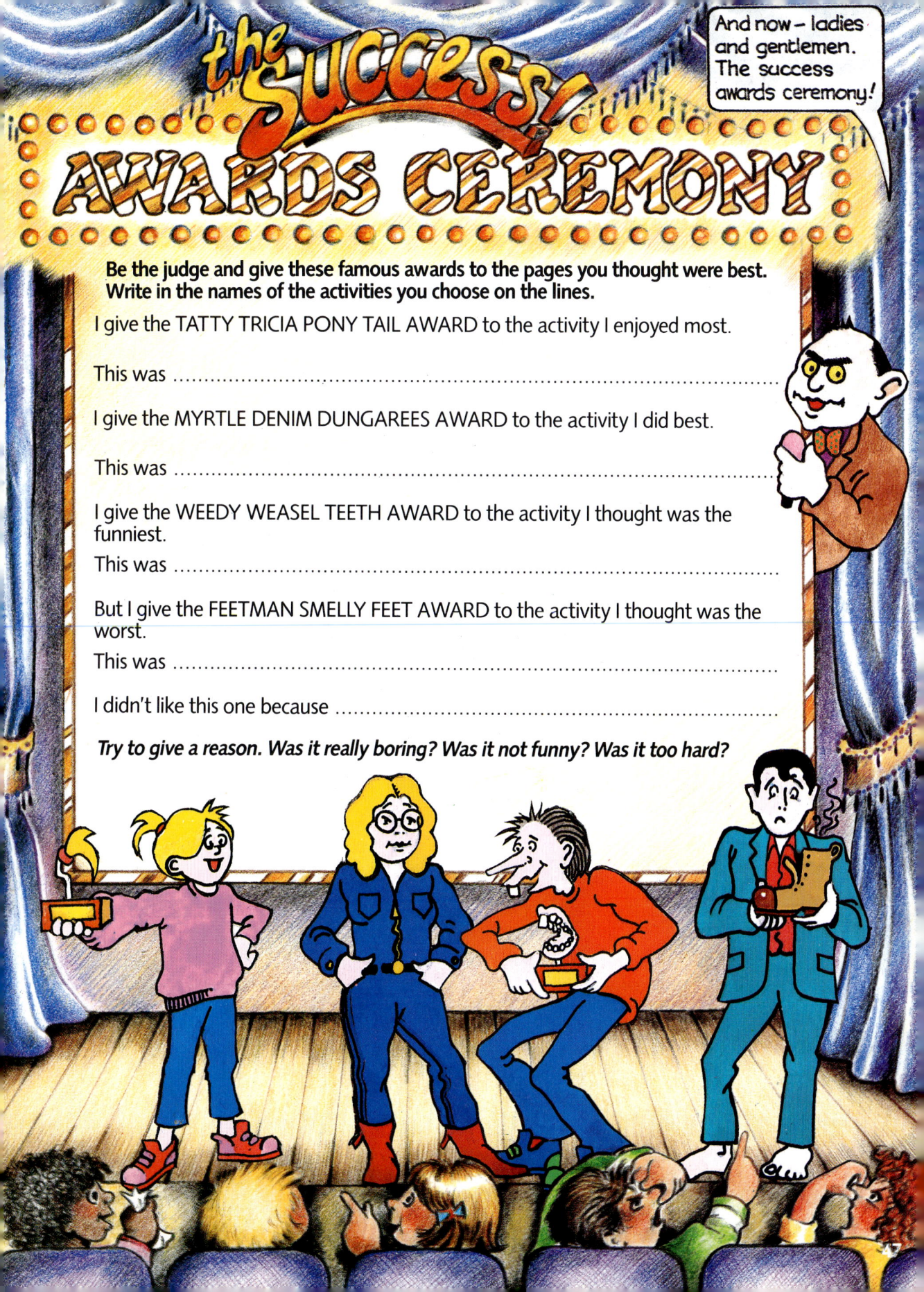

And now – ladies and gentlemen. The success awards ceremony!

Be the judge and give these famous awards to the pages you thought were best. Write in the names of the activities you choose on the lines.

I give the TATTY TRICIA PONY TAIL AWARD to the activity I enjoyed most.

This was ....

I give the MYRTLE DENIM DUNGAREES AWARD to the activity I did best.

This was ....

I give the WEEDY WEASEL TEETH AWARD to the activity I thought was the funniest.

This was ....

But I give the FEETMAN SMELLY FEET AWARD to the activity I thought was the worst.

This was ....

I didn't like this one because ....

Try to give a reason. Was it really boring? Was it not funny? Was it too hard?

SUCCESS!
means GREAT IDEAS

❝ *The very best educational process lies in a confident partnership between child, parents and teachers.* ❞

Success! gives you the chance to make your contribution as effective as possible. We provide a range of imaginative opportunities for you to select from. They can be combined in different ways to achieve the progress you are looking for.

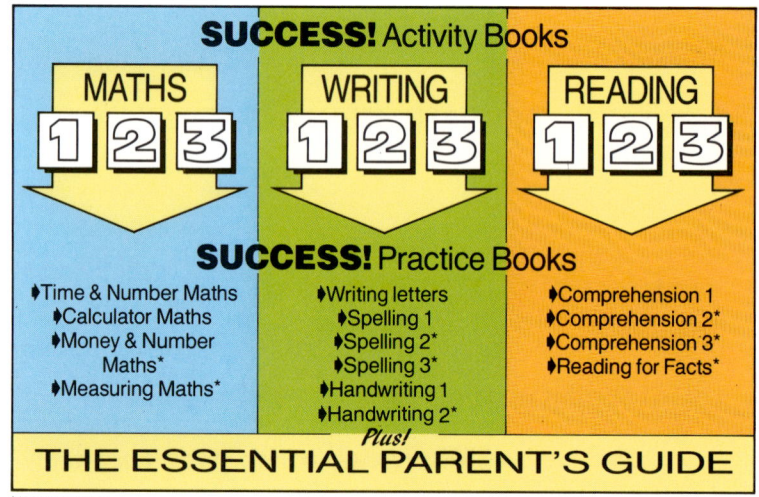

SUCCESS! Activity Books

MATHS 1 2 3 | WRITING 1 2 3 | READING 1 2 3

SUCCESS! Practice Books

- Time & Number Maths
- Calculator Maths
- Money & Number Maths*
- Measuring Maths*

- Writing letters
- Spelling 1
- Spelling 2*
- Spelling 3*
- Handwriting 1
- Handwriting 2*

- Comprehension 1
- Comprehension 2*
- Comprehension 3*
- Reading for Facts*

Plus **THE ESSENTIAL PARENT'S GUIDE**

* in preparation

SUCCESS! *activity books*

This book is only one of nine activity books covering Maths, Writing and Reading. These books provide challenging and attractive exercises in the *whole business* of the main subjects.
You can choose the subject or subjects that you think particularly need help, and start with the first Level in each one to see how much progress can be made.

SUCCESS! *practice books*

This is a series of books designed to improve specific skills which are part of the whole business of each subject. The exercises are easier than the Activity Books, but they are still lots of fun to do. They concentrate on building ability and confidence in the basic tools everyone needs to be good at the subjects.